Letters Ain't Written Adams Alriano

Letters ain't Written

Adams Alriano

Published by BONGO TIMES NOW, 2024.

LETTERS AIN'T WRITTEN

First edition. March 8, 2024.

ISBN: 979-8224161317

Written by Adams Alriano.

Table of Contents

the mind taught me love,

To the hands that cradled my heart,

To the eyes that beheld my pain,

To a heart that cared for my feelings,

To you, my beloved of the heart.

1

2

LETTERS AIN'T WRITTEN

BY ADAMS ALRIANO.

3

LOVE STORY

"Once upon a time, She is called Mona,

his longtime friend, the beloved of his soul.

Personally, he called her the flower of the desert, the anticipated queen of the Toda kingdom before they parted on Davy's journey to seek the value of his death, when he who was an obedient famous poet slave within ancient Thebes.

They didn't communicate even when they wrote letters, none of which reached their intended recipient. Their thoughts spoke together as they struggled for the true meaning of life while immersed in the profound mystery of love,

their destiny hanging in the balance of Love and Fear.

I learn how they talk in dreams, and I overheard their conversation before one of them said that love enhances strength and capabilities twofold. Before I said love weakens the strong and destroys the weak. But then I knew someone who loves unconditionally, his love has never end.

He is the one and only"

From the novel, **A queen from Slavery. By Adams Alriano.**

LETTERS AIN'T WRITTEN

To the mind taught me love,
To the hands that cradled my heart, To the eyes that beheld my pain,
To a heart that cared for my feelings, To you, my beloved of the heart.

ADAMS ALRIANO

"I wish I could heal the wounds of my word world, the world of
unwritten poems I know,
Poems my heart wrote in my dreams I dream on the cage of fear.
When I miss the best version of myself and everyone I killed on my
expectations, I wish I could live the life I hate."
-Davy's Mona
(Traveler on the emotional death journey.)

PREFACE

If love were a journey, the narrative of Davy in "A Queen from Slavery" could serve as a poignant metaphor.

This story unfolds the life of a young boy who willingly becomes a slave out of love for his mother. Selling himself to settle his master's debt and secure freedom for his family.

Davy is separated from his beloved Mona, the pharaoh's daughter. While in slavery, he receives a disheartening message that Mona is engaged and seemingly indifferent to his existence despite the possibility of securing his freedom with pieces of silver.

Davy grapples with his emotions, writing numerous letters that never truly express his deep-seated feelings.

Every soul is a witness to the pains of love, every heart that was ready to love encountered unexpected pain.

It might be true that when you choose the journey of love, you choose to sacrifice everything, including your happiness, to protect another soul, a soul that may care little about you when it should be the one caring and valuing by you the most.

"What is the true concept of love?

Why do the pains not leave in a life filled with abundance of suffering and a small pearl of comfort?

What mistake makes the heart enter into pain every sunrise? Why do memories not fade away? Is it true that I am not lucky?"

These questions and many others he asked when he lacked the right words to write in his letter to Mona.

He blamed himself for many decisions he made, but nothing changed.

So, just like the word love, such a very popular term worldwide believed to be the most powerful word, human life is filled with joy and abundance, as well as the pains that come with love struggles.

Every heart needs to possess a kind of love it requires.

Love weakens; love empowers the weak to become stronger; love molds every difficult word into creation.

Although everyone has their own meaning of the word 'love'

if, for you, love is prioritizing the needs of what you like and its value before yours, then you should read these messages and compositions that immerse you in the world of emotions.

I hope this unwritten letter will give you the chance to explore within yourself and find answers to all your questions about love.

-Adams Rabbit Alriano Letters Ain't Written.

LETTERS AIN'T WRITTEN

TABLE OF CONTENTS

CHAPTERS

9

CHAPTER 01

NIGHTMARE SHADOWS

'Memory is a way of holding on to the things you love, the things you are, the things you never want to lose."

— Kevin Arnold

There's a mystery I never thought would be my life, I'm unaccustomed to sleeping in dreams I never had. Taken by dreams of a warrior in death land,

A battle that rejects the frailty of emotions and the poets of thoughts as I once was,

Before I recognized the value of my journey.

(The saddest poem I read)

ADAMS ALRIANO

ALL OF MY MEMORIES

They said, Memories in the brain are written and erased repeatedly; I cannot deny it. It may be true,

But for me to believe, I need to witness A bullet of ink inside a pencil, inscribing within the mind

And the eraser which erases the beauty of words.

There are times I confine my mind By closing its eyes of thought Contemplating these emotions

While still feeling its touch upon my heart.

I gaze at my heartbeats when you were in front of me, When you embraced my hand tightly.

I felt colder than ice frozen in my hands. My fingers intertwined with yours

To the point of tasting a new flavor of love

As I gazed upon the sky painting your radiant smile In that luminous evening.

My heartbeats changed,

It pounded so fast that it even altered my breath,

Making me pant as if I were in a realm I had never been before, The day we first fell in.

LETTERS AIN'T WRITTEN

"The more you can remember, the more you can learn."
— Buckminster Fuller

15

ADAMS ALRIANO

I long for the days when we were in love, When you called
me sweetheart, honey? My love, My butterfly.

16

LETTERS AIN'T WRITTEN

I read the ancient epic in my language,

What language should rule my throat, binding me to silence the feelings of my heart?

Is it loneliness language?

The shattered heart of a hereon, my queen,

Please open up and receive the verses of my patience.

I am in servitude, obedient to my master,

Not the slavery of love that once bound my life, but the real enslavement of the payment for the poverty of my family's hope.

If you lay eyes on her, hold her hands, and look into her face, Speak my words written on this paper, let her know how I remember her on the battlefield.

I miss everyone on my own planet,

I think of her on every moment of my death.

-How're Doing dear Mama.

ADAMS ALRIANO

If I were an exact time traveler,
An athlete, traversing backward through time, And forward,
as I wish,
I would return to the moments we first met, I would see in
what manner
The future lies before us,
Unveiling its mysteries and possibilities In a way only time
can reveal.

I would see the one who made numerous promises, Swearing
never to leave me,

Now distant, unaware of my whereabouts, No interest in
knowing anything about me.

The one who professed love repeatedly, Claiming it wouldn't
be the same without me, Now finds joy with someone else,

If only I had known that you would change one day, I
wouldn't have allowed closeness.

I would have kept my distance,

Just as we were when we were strangers.

LETTERS AIN'T WRITTEN

I was so timid, couldn't even call you by your name,

I was too young in love, never expressing my love verbally though it was there.

Not because I didn't want to, I did, but my lips were heavier, I was very shy.

I remember everything, I remember that love.

-When she so was young

Everything changed right after being apart,

Even love has its limits too, if it began, there will be a time it will live.

No need to force a love that's not ready to stay, Let it go, someone better will come along,

Did you ever think there might be a time to meet them?

Or that one day you would love someone as you did before? It's always like that.

Although our eyes cannot allow us to read every word on the front page of our lives,

Nothing more valuable will endure forever.

I know how hard it is, but you can forget everything,

Do you wonder how easily they seem to have forgotten about you? Or maybe they never loved you as much as you did?

No need to hold onto that pain,

It doesn't prove you have true love.

Love starts with you, begin by loving yourself, Give it what it needs right now.

Let them go.

(I felt my brain speaking to me)

I can't believe the time I predicted has already come, your heart has already changed.

21

Anyway, deny, accept, don't trust me. But that's not important for now.
I want to remind you something,

Back when I told you that the love you have will end, you were not ready to accept, and you said it would never happen. You believed you would never leave this journey.

Would you tell me where you are now?

LETTERS AIN'T WRITTEN

Is it love?

In the moments of joy,

Your hearts were woven together,

Two souls dancing, love captivatingly crafted.

In the darkness of sorrow, hand in hand you walked Facing
the storm, tears gently fell.

But now,
the pain is hitting you alone,
at a time when they are no longer here,
Just busy tending to someone's else feelings.

It's enough now; you shouldn't wait for something that
won't come back as you used to when they left and returned.

They are not where you were,

the time when you threw a flower up, it either came back,
and you caught it,

or it fluttered a bit in the wind and fell to the side, and you
picked it up.

This is another planet, the planet of sorrow and pain,
A planet where anything that leave your hand goes away
forever and farther,

It cannot return because there is no force of attraction to keep it close to you,

And there is no gravitational force to make it fall as you were used to;

It is vanishing away the atmosphere.

You've become so lonely,

with no one appreciating you more.

Once, you felt more beautiful than a daisy, attracting all kinds of butterflies,

nor did they make you lonely as you are now.

They fluttered around you as if oblivious to other flowers. Look, you've dried up, not just wilting,

and no butterfly comes to you.

And even if they come, they can't stay because you've changed your perspective and no longer trust anyone.

You've been cast away here, on a planet that's so hard to leave. You'll live here forever until the day you find leaves and thrive again.

If you still believe; you won't thrive forever, this will be the end of your love life.

(Letter to my heart)

LETTERS AIN'T WRITTEN

No one loves you more than your heart,
giving it everything when you need to feel loved.

No one cares for you more than your mindset,
speaking to you every time you need help before someone by
your side.

No one values you more than your hands,
providing you with everything you need and keeping it close
to you.

For what do you need more that you can't get yourself,
there's no need to give someone your heart, live your life and
love your own fate

LETTERS AIN'T WRITTEN

It's true, you love each other, they love you, and you love them even more.

But there is no bliss between you;
each one is in pain because of the other.
And neither of you wants to be apart even for a moment.

What is the value of these loves?

If it brings you pain, there's no need to continue embracing it, even if it is love.

Why love knows nothing more than giving its possessors pain or joy.
Decide now what you need in that love.

Jealousy hurts the most when you need your space alone, and it's given freely to someone else.

Unfortunately, you discover that even though they did everything for you, you were just a backup plan, and someone else got more than you ever imagined.

Just as planets were surrounded by their orbits when your love encircled my life, I had no jealousy because each planet had only one orbit. Everything fell apart after another orbit, not mine, was given a chance.

Perhaps this is my first time witnessing someone having more than one friend and giving them all equal time.

There are moments when they give more space to one and forget the other without even realizing that changes are happening.

There's no need to blame,
Find fault, and hurt someone more, If it's not out of love.
Learn to speak the truth;
You should have been transparent, And explained everything.

Everyone should acknowledge, The reality of love.
Indeed, you have the freedom, To love anyone in this world.

But give me a chance to ask you a question,

How can you love someone else, while you did not show love to the one you were with?

You've been with them for a longer time, But until you leave,

You never showed what love truly is.

You can't care about the clothes on your skin, And desire something new; it's not that easy.

Even if you have another in the future, you won't recognize its value and will abandon it for another.

LETTERS AIN'T WRITTEN

Why pretend not to understand,
blaming me every day for things you know the origin of?
Every day,

I've been the one to start conversations between us, and if I
don't, we wouldn't talk,

and then you blame me for being too busy. It's okay; I'm
ready to receive those blames.

Perhaps you don't even realize that there's someone you love
more, or maybe you're afraid to seem ready to have lost the
game from the start by loving someone else.

You lose interest in me.

Don't worry because I know that,
So, there's no need to stay and burden yourself.

Don't force your heart to seem to care about something that
isn't the purpose of your emotions.

Be free, I also acknowledge it's not your fault to change the
direction of the winds of your love.

Use a time that you could use to nurture your new love,
then there's no point in lingering more and giving you much
stress.

You planted a seed with hopes that a plant would sprout, not knowing exactly how it would grow. It's possible it may not grow, even if you water it every day; not every plant that dies lacks water.

The plant sprouted, and slowly it began to grow. You were supposed to care for it and provide everything essential for it to thrive and attract more butterflies.

However, you no longer do this after falling for a flower more attractive than the seed you planted yourself.

Have you ever wondered what would happen if you stopped caring? It's true that the flower may die, as many do when neglected, not because they can't take care of themselves, but because they are influenced by habits.

That's why not all of them die; some just wither for a while, then adapt and start thriving on their own.

Who cares for the plants growing in vast forests or on mountaintops? They live more peacefully without a caretaker, and they become even more resilient than those receiving care.

I hope you can comprehend that there will be occasions when I'll need love, though not consistently.

The time will come when I am distant and liberated from this love prison where I endure ceaselessly.

I assure you; I won't be vulnerable to love any longer. PROMISES

Why is it no longer by your side, what you said you would love forever and protect more than your life?

Why doesn't that love present anymore, the love you believed would endure within you even beyond your death?

Do you recognize what caused everything to change as it was before?

Do you think you can own it again, or is there a time you might lose it unexpectedly as it was at the beginning?

If you don't take the time to learn and understand the reasons behind your past pain,

Your emotions will carry you and thrust you back into where you felt you could escape, because you change your heart.

If you don't know why, then you will hurt every day, even when your heart seems to be numb.

Everything changed when I started loving you, unfortunately,

I made you realize this too early by expecting you to care and give me more space than you naturally would, without knowing that I already loved you more.

I didn't know that I was welcoming pain and entering a game I couldn't play even once.

I didn't know that love would make me this weak; every day my head felt heavy with thoughts I couldn't bear alone, especially when there was no one to help me carry them.

There are times when I believe you know what I'm going through and understand how you can pull me out of this slowly consuming planet of my heart.

I've stayed here like a fool, waiting to see water freeze under the scorching heat of the sun.

I feel every day thinking about things that are impossible, and I don't have the capability to fight for that love, so I have no choice but to accept losing, even if it's true that I need it.

But why hurt me this much?

Are you doing this because I said I have a rock heart? If that's the case, there's no need to continue with the game.

Let's end it here.

I've already accepted that I am weak. Thank you also for making me realize that.

Without fighting in battle, the queen would not have known the weakness of her army. But now, she can strengthen her kingdom, and it will not be weak as it once was. 37

(Kingdom Of Love)

No one cares more about your heart than you do.
If you take it from the center of your chest and give it to
someone else,
they can break it at any time,
especially when they find another heart that cares.

Thank you, Bee. I learned something from you.

Every corner of the land and sky,

on the left and the right, the east and the west. Every morning and night, sunrise and sunset, through the rainy and dry seasons, Every second, they are.

Things that bring us more pain than reasons for joy in our lives.

Even if we were supposed to seek our happiness,

They were still there to make us lose it and witness us returning to where we started,

In intense and unparalleled pain.

CHAPTER 02

STRUGGLES WE MADE

"I've found that luck is quite predictable. If you want more luck, take more chances.

Be more active. Show up more often"

-Brian Tracy

A slave,

This is also the poet's name.

Since that time when he was bound by pain, struggling to unravel the mysteries of the love of his people, when he failed to prepare his own planet.

Although he is not sterile like other slaves,
He still has hope of claiming the prize of victory for his chains.

His promises of true love in his old memories have never faded; he awaits the time to write the meaning of his verses about the mountains of purpose and the emotions of hope."

I still feel my memories burning my emotions, reminding me of how my lips once declared that tears would never fall from my eyes because of love.

It would indeed have never happened if I had continued to live the life I was used to and not played other games that I had never played before.

Yes, I entered the dangerous game by giving my heart to others and providing them with the reasons for my joy.

Consequently, a lot of pain filled the pool of emotions in my heart.

I have shattered even my own heart and handed it over to someone else.

I broke it and placed the pieces in front of me. I don't know how I will return to my old self.

Not only have I let down those I promised, but I also feel ashamed for my own heart.

I wonder what I will say to them to make them understand. I didn't know that entering this would only bring a pill of happiness, but also unparalleled and intense pain.

We had so many plans back then, which have turned into mere dreams, not the kind of dreams we thought would come true.

You said you would love to go to Thebes, where we would have the best time enjoying our love.

I remember promising to spend our time together, introducing me to all the people you wanted to meet.

I don't want to believe that only one of all our dreams come true. Back when I wished to have you with me all night, holding and never letting go, look now, I sleep with you every day, I walk with you every second.

It's you, whose smile never fades whenever I look at you. You are the one who refuses to be far from me, even when there's something you need at a time when I can't provide.

You're always present in a picture I can't leave at home because I feel you would be very lonely without me all the time.

I do always sleep with your picture until I see you.

"Your pictures, Beautiful paintings, all those we painted
together back then,

the ones that left with my hands.
They are searching for their second artist, asking me where the second
rib is?
The one sketched together with me."
-The sand we draw

ADAMS ALRIANO

The battles are not yet over;

I await the end of this journey.

There is no room for another love as long as memories still linger in the mind of the lonely and vulnerable lover.

If the heart is to accept another before letting go of the one who entered first, then this is the time when the pain will cease without either side knowing how it happened.

LETTERS AIN'T WRITTEN

Like I burned your love letter and kept the ashes in a locket around my neck every day, believing that there will be a time to bring it back to life.

Maybe you've taken everything from them, or they make you feel like I'm not suitable for you.

I won't say I have no jealousy,

Not because I fear to look like I am devoid of true love, or I don't care at all.

I struggle to make my heart not compare anything with someone else, not to compare what I got with what anyone close to you is receiving in this time when I'm not near you.

Most importantly,

I'll express gratitude and thank you for the slice of love I received from you.

(Thanksgivings)

MY FAITH

I believe our love will have no end, no matter what happens.

I am ready for the battles and prepared to defend this love until the end of my life because,

whether you grow with me or you are ready to leave, I am committed to being with you.

My Dearest,

I wish I knew how to swim, dive into your mind, keeping it away from thinking of leaving me alone in this world of sorrow and loneliness that craves the warmth of your fingers to hold mine.

I'll live the worst life, though I won't be dead, I'll live longer than the dead.

It's like the dead who came back to life and didn't have memories.

I won't care about my life because I did everything for myself when I learned to love my soul from you, you loved my soul more than myself, and you gave me the real meaning of love.

Before you leave,
I love you much, dear Loml.

Despite the long moments of sadness, Each encounter brought a smile,
Making us forget the pains we had gone through.

I recall the times when you used to tease me, Especially after giving me a hug,

Claiming you had never done that before.

We loved to stay among the rocks,

hard rocks resembling our love at that time,

a love that covered many conflicts and made our eyes unaware of the end of this journey.

Since you left,
I walk alone again,
Afraid even to climb the mountain, Fearful of revisiting more memories,
The ones from the time when we were together,
Afraid they might turn my day into one filled with sorrow.

You made me love what I hate at this moment.

I am not ready to write you letters like all those I wrote when we were together, at a time when my tears didn't change anything.

How will it be this time?

LETTERS AIN'T WRITTEN

Show me the end of the sky,
Give me a count of the stars and tell me the weight of the clouds.

Why did you decide to deceive, you were never real, not even once.

You made me believe in impossible things when you said you would take the sunlight and bring it into the thick darkness of the forest of sorrows when I am alone.

I just struggle alone,

Why don't I see you anymore,

And you're not here when I need you?

Maybe I should believe you did everything because the one you needed couldn't provide what you needed back then.

When you thought you could get it from me more easily without even exerting much effort to explain what you needed.

Indeed, you used me to find your own happiness, you used my heart without being ready to provide yours for me.

Lomly,

Love is true and real,
Regardless of gender or feelings, It cannot be denied,
If someone spends enough time with you, They will eventually develop love.

If there's no compelling reason to keep them close,

It's better to limit the time spent together to protect our love, Avoiding unnecessary stress,

I'll do everything as you wish,

And if I can't, feel free to do it with someone else.

(retro feelings)

You were with me during the time he claimed to genuinely love me,

Saying he couldn't be far from me.

He promised to protect the value of my love for him, If I reciprocated as he loved me.

Did you not know that one day he would change?

Did you not realize he might have been lying when he said he was unhappy without me,

While he seemed to be thriving every day, posting happily on social networks?

I'm afraid to even look at his posts now, as they only intensify my resentment.

If you knew, why didn't you say anything and let me continue loving him?

And if you didn't know, why did you accept being part of his oath? I ask for answers.

(A letter to flowers)

Have you ever thought about how it would be, if one day you discovered that everything,

they did for you was just to deceive you, and they never genuinely loved you even once?

They used your love to manipulate and make you vulnerable, unable to see what would come after your love story.

What if they were doing it as revenge for all the pain you caused in their life?

(a mindset of pawn poker)

LETTERS AIN'T WRITTEN

PRETTIEST PETTY,

I am not sure if it's really you,

the one who cared about a tiny piece of paper with the word 'I love you' written on it.

The one who didn't be ready to go anywhere without hearing that word from the tongue of a weak servant.

I am not sure if this is the person who today forgets that they were supposed to meet me.

A time when you eagerly waited for me to be the first to say, "I love you," and your response would come later, not with a simple "thank you,"

but with an insistence that everyone should know.

I'm surprised that every time I want to meet you, you bring up many reasons why we can't,

while in those days when you loved me deeply, you were not willing to let me go for a moment.

I understand an ending that everyone foresaw, a time when I believed nothing would change,

and I thought I would still have your heart forever. I feel I haven't left anything for you.

If there's anything you need me to do for the last time before you allow me to leave your life, then tell me what to do now.

There are times when suffering becomes so intense, to the point where help seems elusive,

You find yourself in a vast desert with terrifying storms and scorching heat.

Even if you have enough water to nourish the small baobab tree you planted,

Hoping it would one day provide shade to alleviate the pain of the intense sun, you may still perish without enjoying the fruits of your labor.

There are moments when the only decision left is to succumb to despair and leave, seeking a baobab tree whose planter has long passed, choosing to rely on it rather than summoning the courage within to endure something that offers no solace in your life.

-Awareness

"Survival of the fittest is not about the strongest, but those most responsive to change."

- Charles Darwin

LETTERS AIN'T WRITTEN

It's been a long time since I last gazed into your beautiful eyes,

I believe you've grown and changed significantly. My memories take me back to the time when we were believers in the same temple, at the time we all believed we could live forever.

We exchanged letters as if we were people who hadn't seen each other in years, even though we were together every day.

It's been more than four years now, but I doubt if I can forget your last letter.

I've kept it to read whenever I need to hear your voice or reminisce about your smile,

before I changed the picture you left me with,

so, it would be easier for me to carry it in the locket around my neck.

(Hello my oldest feeling)

My feelings compel me to believe that the last time I saw you, that day before I bid farewell without saying goodbye for real. My greatest fear was about you; I feared how I would wipe away your tears when you see mine falling to the ground.

62

I don't mean to portray them as weak or junks, but this is the
reality;

They are nothing more than me.

You've given them the chance likely precious, possessing
everything more than I do.

Perhaps they have everything you need,
but they cannot perform with excellence as I did when we
were together.

It's akin to a butterfly waiting to emerge from its chrysalis,
only to live a shorter time,

Missing the type of flower,

it hoped to meet when it hasn't yet seen the world devastated
by human destruction.

That's how you'll blame yourself after everything crumbles,
realizing they are not what you wished them to be,

when you discover the essence of what I meant to you,
despite my many flaws that you were already aware of and
could have controlled,

You'll long to return to me, but you won't find that chance.

ADAMS ALRIANO

You're flitting about,

unable to see me because I didn't need you either.

You departed that night when I needed you, and now you've returned to the daytime,

a time when the sun has already risen.

I no longer need your aid; the sunlight is enough to bring me joy. I don't need happiness from anyone else because soon enough, I'll be able to find my own happiness.

(Poor bat)

LETTERS AIN'T WRITTEN

I'm sorry, Alrenado,

I know you love me, and I love you too.

But I can't continue this relationship with you.

I know you'll have many questions and want to know why.

I also wish to tell you everything, but I don't want to burden you with heavy thoughts.

Let me deal with everything myself because it concerns me more. I'm hurting a lot, and I can't stop this pain,

but you need to understand that I'm doing this for you, and the main reason is my family.

I love you so much, and I wish you all the best in your new relationships.

-Broken Queen

ADAMS ALRIANO

Close your eyes; I want to give you a gift. It's uniquely beautiful, and
believe me, it's something you'll love,
not what you might be thinking.
(Nothing)

66

I've seen many people in relationships, and not even one among them is happy.

I've seen many who deeply care for each other but never got the chance to be together.

I've seen even more people who completely disbelieve in love because, for them, it has never brought meaning.

Yet, I still feel that none of them have pain greater than those who initially planted joy using love and later reaped the harvest of pain.

People like I, a traveler of my own loneliness planet.

A strong wind swept through, pushing a branch of the tree, and a leaf fell from where it once clung to the ground.

There, it joined many other leaves, either dropped by the wind or fallen due to their own weakness, unable to continue holding on as they once did when they loved the tree,

that love weakened them. None of them can return, even if given the chance; everything ended there.

I was to feel compassion, but I still had to contemplate more about the leaves that fell due to the tree itself during the dry season.

Did they not deserve to?

Why did they endure staying, and how did the tree not carry them and decide to cast them away?

Before I see myself like these leaves, no longer having the value I once did when I was the reason the tree looked more beautiful than others.

Now, I seem to have no purpose other than making it look worse by chasing away beautiful butterflies and causing it to lose its water.

Perhaps the mistake is mine for perceiving love the way I wanted to see it, and not as the world does.

(Leaf spoken)

LETTERS AIN'T WRITTEN

I've missed you so much, and I don't even understand why I
miss you this much.

Is it because of love alone?

Every day feels more intense than the last, and
I can't stop my mind from thinking more about you. I wish I
could see you,
but I don't know when or where that will happen. If I could
control it,
I wouldn't have let you go this far away from me.

"Why did you agree to let them go so far, and why didn't you stay with them and go where they went?"

Every day my heart asks me this question, and I haven't found an answer to give.

I can't hide how much I hate these life circumstances.

I am a slave, I know it's all because of poverty,

and if not for that, we wouldn't have these lives that keep us so far apart.

Look, I'm left only to gaze at old pictures of you, pictures that don't even capture the reality of your current face.

I still believe there will be a day when everything will be okay, and I will be close to you, my love. Soon, I will make it in the name of love.

"Let love and faithfulness never leave you; bind them around your neck, write them on the tablet of your heart. Then you will win favor and a good name in the sight of God and man."

Proverbs 3:3-4 (NIV)

I have come back to love you again;

I promise to love you more than yesterday.

I recognize how I hurt your heart with my foolishness, never respecting you even once;

I added and did anything I felt like without caring about the consequences.

I admit I was foolish, that's why I have returned to ask for your forgiveness.

Please forgive me because initially, I didn't know what love is, nor did I understand what pain feels like.

But now I understand everything, and I am not willing to see you in tears again because of love.

I will do everything I can, and even if I can't, I will make sure I do it for you.

If that happens, I will make you the happiest woman in the world one day.

I promise.

LETTERS AIN'T WRITTEN

I KNEW I WAS.

I cannot say the grand reason for everything unraveling was the fame I once had,

nor was it due to my proximity to those who didn't wish our relationship to endure.

I recall just one thing;

I believe this is the root of it all.

When I began to believe I was the choice of every woman in the world,

That's when everything started to shift.

I allowed my heart to be an open book for anyone in need; I thought by doing so,

I would earn accolades from my friends.

Little did I know, I was undermining my own love. Now, I find myself foolish,

no longer understanding the essence of love,

and anyone who comes close to me suffers on my behalf. I've lost touch with the meaning of love, uncertain of its significance in my life.

Someone told me;
"If we never learn to be alone, we will always feel lonely"

74

Before you contemplate deceiving anyone for the sake of love, Within your own soul; Ask yourself if you would be willing to undergo the same,

and if it were to happen,

how you would react before going ahead with your decisions. Never deceive another soul before deceiving your own heart; You deluded yourself first, and that's why you deserve to be deceived as well.

Every day you lament they are not always there when you need them,
Yet you claim to love them even if they do not reciprocate.

Now, what kind of love is that?

It's not love but rather forcing their soul to love you. If you genuinely love them, you will do everything for their sake, even if they do nothing for you.

You should give them freedom to choose,
what they need, and what they love so that they can find their happiness.

Manure is not used by rabbits but by sunflowers, Flowers are not for sunflowers; they are for bees.

Because even honey is not for bees, they make it themselves but cannot consume it,

Although they don't use anything extraordinary, they protect it day and night so that if anyone tries to take it, they stand strong.

Love is not for yourself but for someone else, but because it comes from within you,

You must create it within yourself first and ensure you protect it. You shouldn't give it to everyone because its value is greater than how others perceive it.

Love yourself first, date your own soul before anyone else, as you know yourself better than anyone else. Once you know how to love yourself more, you won't struggle to love anything and appreciate it, as you have learned from your own soul.

Today I saw someone dressed like you,

wearing over-sized clothes just the way you like, and from a distance, she walked as you would.

I look to see where her preferences would satisfy me,

hoping that by doing so, I would find joy in watching someone resembling the one I lost for an exceptionally long time.

However, it turned out not to be the case; instead, I was only fueling my memories,

thinking increasingly about you.

I longed so much for it to be truly you, but my desires remained just desires, and not a single thing had changed.

-I miss you already

HAVE A REST

It has been an exceedingly long time since you passed, and I longed so much to see you.

You left with a little comfort that made me appreciate this worldly life.

There wasn't a day I thought you would leave, leaving everyone who loved and cared for you in such sorrow and intense suffering.

Your siblings are praying for you to find a peaceful resting place where you've gone ahead.

I also wish for the time to come when we can be happy together again, as we used to be.

I always believe that the day I met you again, I would be happier,

reliving the moments we once shared.

I won't blame you for shattering my dream, uprooting even the small leaf I planted,

I hope it will bloom for me one day.

Fragile butterfly, you broke my wings, preventing me from flying beside you.

When I wished to embrace you and express how much I remembered you, you were busy with other things and didn't seem to care about anything.

You just forced me to believe that indeed you never loved me; you just needed something from me, and that's why you deceived me.

-All I know

ADAMS ALRIANO

Tell me just one word,
Have you already found all you need?
Is there still something you need from me?

Tell me to leave and never return to your life. I know you no longer need anything,

So, it's better you stop hurting me.

I believe there are many more butterflies that will need me again, and I understand that one day,

I will find a friend even better than you.

Someone who will love me and understand the value of love.

(Tears do smile)

For I never knew that one day I would find a friend like you, who would be with me for a noticeably abbreviated time and make me happy.

Then I should believe that there will come a time when someone appears for me,

and I will no longer lament for love.

"Above all, keep loving one another earnestly, since love covers a multitude of sins."

- Bible, 1 Peter 4:8

I longed to see your smiling face every moment I was near you. I wished to feel your need for me close to you again as it was in those times.

I longed for you to call me as you used to when we were together.

However, everything has changed.

You have changed, becoming someone new, not the one I used to cook delicious meals for.

Since, you wanted to see how happy I was while eating.

CHAPTER 03

WHAT IS IT?

"Love didn't hurt you.
Someone who doesn't know how to love hurt you.
Don't confuse the two."

– Jay Shetty

I wish I could have asked myself the question earlier than anything that happened, **what is love?**

Love made me easily dive into relationships, knowing only their small plans and not their values and dreams.

When they changed,

I realized it wasn't love but desire to love.

"Neither butterfly that I'll ask about the most attractive color, nor bees that I'll interrogate about a pleasant scent,

because I don't need the best flower but to know how to love the flower."

-Me

We learn how to love from the environment we were raised in, the people we meet, and our personal beliefs about love.

When someone says, 'I love you,'
it may not mean the same thing as it does for someone else.

The word might signify their presence in your life for one night, their commitment to ensuring you receive everything you deserve.

Conversely, it could mean confining you to a cage, where they exist too, preventing you from being close to anyone else, and making them the center of your life by depending on them. And that's the real heartful slavery.

Love is not about Choose people who choose you. But putting someone needs before yours,

In my own planet, love is being willing to give anything for the smile of another,

to protect it more than your own place in their heart.

Yes, you may either call it a sacrifice or sacred gift.
-Planet Toda Love theories

ADAMS ALRIANO

"Love is patient, love is kind. It does not envy, it does not boast, it is not proud. It does not dishonor others, it is not self-seeking, it is not easily angered, it keeps no record of wrongs. Love does not delight in evil but rejoices with the truth. It always protects, always trusts, always hopes, always perseveres."

1 Corinthians 13:4-7 (NIV)

I cherished and protected the space for someone who acted
against me;
(The mistake i made)

I once believed love was a feeling,

Yet it's not merely a play of emotions but a commitment of hearts that recognizes the value of a butterfly in the garden of affection.

-What is it?

I know I will miss you deeply;

I never knew you would leave this early.

But why didn't you tell me you were leaving so that I could stop pretending to be too busy and claim not to have time to talk to you?

Now, I need you, and I realize that I need you as you depart from my life.
I wished you would continue to be there to teach me more about love.

I got so accustomed to you, and in a fleeting time, I began to be more attracted to your humor and jokes that made me forget the pain within me and see myself as someone of value.

Why didn't you teach me how to see my worth without someone being there for me,

instead, you made me need you more to build my self-confidence, only to leave afterwards?

Hello,

I've decided to write this letter because I long to hear even the sound of your voice.

Oh, I'm sorry, I forgot to ask how you're doing.

How are you?

And what about everything around you?

Have you already found someone else to teach, or can I still be your student?

Teach me even through letters, and I'll be more attentive, ensuring I understand you.

Thank you for the past lessons; now, I understand what love is, pain, hatred, and every intruder of love. I know how to deal with them,

and I learned all this from you.

I never thought there would be a day when you would leave and go so far away from me.

If I had known, I wouldn't have let you go in anger even once; I would have ensured to protect your happiness and not be the reason for its loss.

If I had realized there would be a time of change,

I would have spent all the time you were with me making you feel loved.

I would have written more letters than I ever did back then.

I would have given you gifts you could never find from anyone else in the world.

I would have made sure to love you more than I ever loved myself.

Few birds soar above me, and I wonder if they feel anything,
Are they filled with joy or sorrow, like me?

People who glance at me from afar on the roadside are
puzzled, None understands what has befallen me, and no
one cares enough to inquire.

I have become like a fool in the middle of a vast, dried-up
pond, Sitting under a large tree without shade because its
leaves are withered by the sun.

I watch many bees above me, circling their beehive of honey,
Yet, there is nothing around me except cracked earth with a
few dried-up leaves.

I don't know what occupies my mind to the extent that I
struggle to even drink the tear in my hand.

Why didn't I guard my love, even if it brought me no
benefits like bees and honey?

I allowed it to be taken away from my heart, letting it rule as
it pleased.

I become a person who blames my own soul,

Feeling like I'm creating a small amount of comfort when I'm
increasing the levels of suffering within me.

it's too late;
I don't see you anymore.
Every day, I call your name, and no one answers; I miss you
so much.

I wish I could speak like a parrot, voice out every feeling in me.

If not, I'd prefer to see in the dark like a bat, to emerge from this love's darkness myself.

Perhaps, I'd be brave enough to carry many thorns on me like a porcupine and cover my ears in the cold like a rabbit, not relying on happiness from others, who often end up causing me pain.

I know you've got love, peace, happiness, and respect. There's someone you communicate with every sec,

They ask if you've eaten, you tell them everything about your day, You believe they love you more, listen to you more than I did, They bring you many gifts every time you meet,

They give you their time, and you reciprocate with yours, They take you to places she never thought of going,

For they are not everything in your life?

What about your promises? I guess she shouldn't remember them at all.

I have written many letters for you as we used to,

You don't show any interest, and I doubt if you can read them,

I know there are many letters you read regularly from the new owner of your heart.

I have stayed here on the mountain to see you coming, waiting for the answers to my letters carried by the wind every day; or haven't they reached where you are?

I'm tired of waiting, but my heart still hopes that one day you will receive my messages and reply to me. I will continue to wait until the stars stop adorning the night sky.

They say I am a slave, and I can't deny it. I am a slave to my emotions,

Bound by chains of love, uncertain of how to break free.

I feel guilty every time I attempt to forget you, how can I erase my promises?

Even if one day my love leaves, the promises will continue to bind me.

I shouldn't make promises anymore; people don't care about what they promise, they just say they'll be there forever and then leave.

Let me be a slave; I have accepted it.

During the harsh cold, you gave me your cloth to wear.

I felt like I was embracing you; it always carried your scent, and I didn't want it to lose that.

I still feel your scent everywhere, making me think you're still with me.

I walked through Thebes and caught a whiff of your perfume. I looked in every direction,

but I didn't see you.

I can't count how many times I told you I love you. It feels like more than the days we spent together. How have you managed to erase those words from your memories and retain only a few spoken by someone else?

Why is it that I still can't forget?

May you teach me how to forget you as you do?

ADAMS ALRIANO

You said you love walking at night.

We walked together when there were very few people on the streets, or none at all.

You told me you loved being with me and had no fear, even though you were scared of dogs along the way.

We played many games while walking, and whenever it got very cold, I would put my sweater around you. In the darkness, you held my hand to ease my fears.

Now, I'm left in the darkness of loneliness, with no one to hold my hand.

I never thought I'd enjoy walking at night, but you made me love it, and now you've left me.

I feel incomplete; thoughts torment my mind, especially when I pass the paths we used to walk or visit places you liked.

I can't eat the food we used to enjoy together; it brings back too many memories.

You've made me hate walking at night. I hate the night we walk,

-I hate the night.

When you loved flowers,
I became the sunlight to help them produce their food and thrive for you.

When you loved chocolate, I turned into milk to enhance their delicious taste in your mouth.

When you loved apples, I removed all the seeds and placed them in the center so you wouldn't have trouble while eating.

When you loved honey, I spoke to the bees to make the honey even sweeter.

For everything you loved, I added double the love just for you.

I believed you wouldn't love as much without me. I still wonder how you managed to love someone else without me bringing them into your life.

Why do they love each other and then hate each other? They come together, and later they part ways.

No one believes in love anymore. Maybe love is not how they perceive it.

In this century, love has become an agreement. They agree to be in a relationship or to love each other, thinking that's true love.

But it's not like that.

There are many things that resemble love.

If you're not careful, you might think it's true love. After a long time passes, pain follows.

You'll realize it wasn't love.

You think you love because you haven't found what you absolutely love, or you believe you can't find it, so you decide to love something else.

Do you think you can decide when to love? What to keep and how to love?

The heart always falls in love at unexpected times, but it hates whenever you choose.

It's not that easy to figure out whether it's desire or pity. Was it love?

I never thought there would be a day when we would be this close.

Not going to sleep without being wished goodnight while wrapped in your embrace.

Even when I go to sleep, I talk to my bed, telling it how wonderful my day was because you were with me all the time.

I struggle to sleep, thinking about all the happy moments we shared.

I don't think there's a place in your mind that you're not aware of, as you've been roaming in my thoughts all day.

You've never had a moment like this before, being told you're loved by someone like me, and you believing in that love.

No one can believe it, a queen and a servant loving each other.

Every time I wonder how this love will last, my heart tells me if it's truly the kingdom of love, there's nothing to bring it down.

ADAMS ALRIANO

WHY

Now I understand why love is blind You've created your own
planet

And you don't know how life goes on outside

You don't believe there can be pain because of love

You've forgotten that there will be times when they won't be
around,

You believe they are everything and you'll be together
forever You don't care about anything from anyone else

I know you're ready to lose everything, even if the entire
world separates you,

You feel like you'll still live with them on your own planet.

I wish you understood what love is.

See how it blinds you, and you don't see what's coming ahead. There will be times when you'll suffer more than you think, with no one by your side.

I feel sorry for you.

Do you ever leave someone for their sake?

Do you feel they could never leave you for someone else? Do you know what they love about you?

Have you ever wondered what would happen if what they love about you were to disappear.

You were brave, a hero, and the strongest.

Everyone looked up to you as a monument because of the many battles you fought.

See how you became weak because of love.

You've become intoxicated with many unanswered thoughts in your mind.

If you don't make decisions soon, you'll lose everything in your life. I watch you live a life you don't like, unable to understand your own feelings.

Yes, that's right, but

It's not always necessary to care much about your feelings; learn to evaluate what is right,

Desires are liars; failing to control them will take away all your life treasures.

When the heart needed, it didn't understand When it understood, it hesitated to believe Even when it believed, it didn't accept the truth Eventually, it accepted, but it still wasn't ready When it was ready, it feared to tell truth

The day it needed to; it realized it was too late

Blame is futile; you wasted time on your own accord.
Nor can you claim misfortune, for everything is within your reach

You could have had that love if you truly desired, and ready for the battle.

You were present in my room last night I saw you with flowers in hand

I felt they were meant for me, but

Before you could hand them over, you left, and I didn't know where you went

Because it was only a dream

"Why did you wake up? If you had lingered in the dream, everything would have been fine"

I felt my heart speaking to me

Then I slept, but I didn't see you again; you were already gone

Look now, you've left again, and I didn't get a chance to bid you farewell
How does it happen that every day I repeat the same mistake?
-Dreams

"If I see you again in my room, I will close the doors and windows so that you have no way out until you give me an answer to my question:

Why do I still think of you this much when you have already left my life?"

"I trust you so much, more than anyone else. I have never trusted anyone to this extent.

I don't know why I trust you this much;

I feel that you are the only one who can understand me in this world."

-Once claimed

If you knew that, why didn't you do something? You allowed me to continue suffering when you could have taken me out of this pain.

Is it because I listened to you so much? Indeed, I trusted you more than anything.

How can I trust you again?

I don't even feel the value of your love anymore. Love seems to know nothing but hurting everyone who cherishes it.

I ~~hate~~ you so much.

(to my heart)

ADAMS ALRIANO

On our first met

Before I discover I liked all of you

I liked your motion, u walked like my brother I liked the way
you talk, polite like my mom I liked the way you act, gentle
like my father

I liked your smell, you smelled like white daisy

I liked your voice, melodious like the tunes of a wooden
flute. I liked your demeanor, serene like a butterfly in the
universe.

I liked your skin, golden-black akin to the Toda horse's
necklace. I loved your words, cherished poetry of a lunar
pharaoh.

If rocks could speak,

they would tell tales of the joy we found whenever we sat upon them,

when you longed to have me by your side in the emotionally charged wind at the summit,

(I acknowledge that someone else may bring you happiness,

but they will never make your smile shine brightly and authentically through your lips.)

If trees and flowers could speak,

they would remind you of all the beautiful words I ever told you when we rested close to them,

(Everybody can talk, but no one could touch your heart with words alone as I did back then.)

If the sky could speak,

then twinkling stars and the moon would recount how enchanting we looked every night under its canopy,

(You were free to express anything when you enjoyed the spectacle of the sky. I understand there are many beautiful things, but none could adorn your life as I did through the beauty of nature.)

When you're happy, you may not recognize what love truly is; everything seems to be in your favor.

It's during challenging times, sadness, grief, suffering, and fear when everything that was once close leaves, when you need help but find none. That the true test of love arises.

If they couldn't give a little when I needed it, the grand gestures during times when I didn't need them won't change my perspective on their love, nor can it deceive me;

I understand this isn't love.

Love is about doing everything, giving everything for everything that means everything in your life.

Giving something when I don't need anything is better than giving to someone who was everything when I meant nothing to them?

(I knew it was)

LETTERS AIN'T WRITTEN

Dearest,

If I am too late and someone else marries you, I will send you many flowers as a gift,

Accompanied by a letter written with red human tissue, I will take it from the hand you loved to hold.

If I happen to attend the venue,

I will sing beautiful songs for you, the songs I used to write before. If I get the chance to choose the type of gift I prefer because my emotionally charged song has brought tears from your eyes;

Then I will choose to be a housekeeper in your home.

I will gaze at your face every day, pretending to my heart,

To keep you by my side, believing that you are mine until death. I don't need to break my promise "I will be with you forever."

You said this often when praising me as a good cook: "On the day I become pregnant, I won't do anything. I will just lie down and wait for you to cook a delicious meal for me and our child."

I will make sure your dream comes true; I will prepare the most delicious meal every day.

I know I won't be able to feed you; someone else will feed you while I am washing dishes or doing household chores.

122

I will make your bed and decorate it with the most beautiful flowers you love. I won't give you chocolate because I won't have the ability to go to the supermarket and buy anything.

I will do all this while in a deep sleep that I won't wake up from after my soul departs.

I know I will endure pain, but it will be challenging to compete with emotions and eventually adapt to this situation.

If he marries you,
I'll die, the Death of the thirsty Buffalo in the Well.

ADAMS ALRIANO

"I know it will cost me a lot to be away from you, my ribs,"

for these were the words you wrote in your final letter. If you don't mind, allow me to ask you a question:

What pain were you talking about?

Why do I see so many pictures of you smiling? Is this not the person who wrote me that letter?

Many questions swirl in my mind without answers. Is it because I am a slave, just a poor boy,

Have those with wealth already bought your heart?

But you never needed wealth than love that much when we were together!

I remember I couldn't give you more than my old cloth, Yet you seemed happier than I expected.

I realize you have bought many valuable things, perhaps that's why you lack anything I ever gave you.

I am left to preserve your words in a letter turned to ashes, along with a picture that haunts me every day, believing that there will be a time when I'll be by your side again.

-Your last letter

Let me believe this dream is just a fleeting night illusion that will never come true even once.

IN THE WINGS OF LOVE.
Today, my name has become a stranger Not just introducing myself,
But I must explain more about who I am every time I write you a letter.

It's okay, let me promise you this time I won't write any more letters to you

Not because someone else won't want me to be close to you again, or because you belong to someone else now.

It's because I won't have anything to write if there's nothing you want to know from me.

I ask for greetings

I know he feels incredibly lucky

Maybe he has everything you need that I didn't have.

Look, he has succeeded in owning your heart and taking my place, And I am no longer valuable for now.

I wish he would realize that I too am genius. You said you would be with me forever, You told me beautiful lies you tell him now,

And then you left me because there was something I didn't have. Isn't it easy to leave him for someone else?

I ask that this be my final request to you;
Please, don't make him feel so valuable and important to you.

Don't sink him into the sea of love and then swim away, leaving him to drown, hurting him as you did to me.

If you genuinely love him, endure everything he doesn't have. There will be a time when he'll get it, and if he doesn't deserve to have it, be content with his situation.

I loved her color; she resembled the almond she gave me every night.

My nickname was changed after falling for hers. Even when she mentioned my name,

she pronounced it differently from others,

She said they spoiled my name by mispronouncing it.

I recognized his presence through her fragrance, although there were times even his friend used it.

She looked into my eyes when I held her hand every time I told her stories.

Her eyes were small due to his emotions,

she didn't seem to have shame or fear within her.

I became so accustomed to her that I could read her letters in her voice.

We had so many moments that brought us closer, because this was more than just friendship.

LETTERS AIN'T WRITTEN

It's quite a common word, with just three letters.

I used to say it regularly, and there was no problem. But the day I planned to say it in front of her,

If I meant it, I couldn't.

I don't know how I failed. My heartbeat accelerated.

Maybe because I had never said this word to any girl before.
I felt an unusual fear; my mouth was very heavy.

-younger self

I felt my blood vessels carrying hot blood under high pressure. Eventually, I decided to leave.

I didn't tell him that I loved him, although he understood.

(she said)

LETTERS AIN'T WRITTEN

I love you, my beloved Alado. I wish everyone knew this.

If I could, I would tell the entire world how much I love you.
I've never loved anyone before until I met you.

I love you so much.

(She insisted)

ADAMS ALRIANO

I AM

I did not express how much I love you the first time I needed to, I needed more confidence to do so,

I started learning to speak in front of many people so I wouldn't be afraid to talk to you again.

Look at me now; I could speak in front of many people because of you.

I am a public speaker.

I didn't have enough money to buy expensive gifts for you, I had to prove how much I loved you,

I decided to be creative, prepared many gifts for you because it was my dream to give you a gift that no one else in the world would ever have,

I had to prepare it myself. This increased my creativity.

I am a designer.

I know how much you loved being sung to,

At that moment, I didn't have the ability to sing, although I learned and recorded a few songs for you, but even when I became a musician, I still felt they weren't up to standard.

I decided to use my creativity and my writing skills to prepare letters and poems as best as I could.

I am a poet.

LETTERS AIN'T WRITTEN

Everyone's dream is to be in a relationship that brings happiness,

I understood that I had to do everything to make you happy all the time; I made sure this happiness came from within me so that you would continue to love me more.

Finally, I discovered my talent for making jokes and easy-going humor. Today, because of this,

I am a comedian.

You told me you liked good stories,

You wished I could tell you a story every time I had the opportunity.

Because I don't like using other people's things, and most importantly, I trust my abilities a lot,

I set aside enough time to learn how to prepare adventures.

I created more stories for you until I realized I had the ability to write them.

I started writing slowly, and finally;

I am an author.

I didn't want to be a liar, and I needed to thank you for doing all these things in my life.

When I realized that the word "thank you" alone was not enough to express the magnitude of my gratitude,

LETTERS AIN'T WRITTEN

I decided to prepare a beautiful gift for you.

All these compositions and many letters I wrote here were written because of the pain of love.

I wrote them at a time when I needed human love desperately, before realizing that there is a place where I can find boundless love, a love greater than human love that I found in my dear ones.

I know you don't know this, but today, I am the real me because of you.

I got everything I have because of love.

Tough times and the pain I've endured in the past, blame, and every decision that tortured my mind have shaped me into who I am today.

I won't be wrong if I say, "I am the product of love." In the name of love.

I never knew the value of love, that's why I didn't guard it.

When you met me, life made us come together and be one. Through love, we carried out many wonderful things.

I never understood why you guard your space so much. Nor do you need anyone else to be closer to me than you. Later, I learned what love is,

And I agreed to protect the value.

There will be times when you still are alone,

Like a dry tree growing in the desert without water. Is this
Courage, Loneliness, or Freedom,

A time when no one cares about you? Very few can endure
these feelings.

Everything is possible; you shouldn't have a dream to die for,
But believe; there will be a day when everything changes.

The desert will become a vast wilderness with good soil and
abundant water.

Although this might be just a dream, what's more? Having
hope to grow again after withering?

Or waiting for death after drying up?"

Sing slowly, with intense emotions in your heart, A beautiful song that heals pain,

Feel the reality of your life, look at what you love most,

And think about what brings you happiness, Have you ever smiled?

For that time is not now? If you have hope,

You can still smile, little angel.

-Beautiful song I know

When you needed food late at night,

I no longer feared the darkness nor knights I dreaded losing
your beautiful smile.

My thoughts painted a picture of you with sad eyes, an angry
face, tired cheeks, and cracked lips—all because you miss the
best food you love.

I then said,
"Wait here, my dearest; I'm going to get something for you."
(Castle memories.)

They said you should not believe me anymore; artist are liars so we're not faithful,

They said I am a chariot; I have many girls on my kingdom,
They said all men think about fame,

I am not the best guy for you.

They insisted on you, soon you are going to cry.

They said I will be bought once, and you will not be close to me again,

I know you understand that am just a slave looking for freedom, not mine but theirs but still I wonder why said;

"I do love him until the chains decay"

BEAUTY OF THE SKY

Such a night,

I am tired of the journey.

I am just chilling on the sailboat, moving to the next side of the lake.

I feel so exhausted.

Let me look at the sky to cool my brain.

Wow, stars are twinkling with a little dim moonlight.

I miss you already,

My thoughts turn back to those days

when I saw the beauty of the sky beside you, tired of slavery works.

We created some story stunts before falling in love with nature.

Yet I love the sky,

I like the moon and its stars.

I once called it the secret of the white daisy.

Don't you remember the story I told you about Davy, A genius who lived in the cage on the moonlight?

ADAMS ALRIANO

I am tired a lot,

I have some joint pains, It's so cold,

And no one is here to hold my hand. No one tells me, "Sorry, Alrian," like you used to do in those days.

It was your dream, My dream.

Yes, our dream,

To spend the whole night together,

talking about something we didn't think of talking about.

Why can't I erase these memories?

I do think that my brain is a little ocean.

When I drew your picture on the white sand at the shore, waves are running from left to right.

How can a picture resist the change?

Still, I see your beautiful smile in my daydreams. I miss you already.

Morning sun rises, gently warming our skin and dispelling the chill of the past night.

Our eyes see pride and joy as they freely gaze upon everything. Finally, it's a new day again.

The morning comes to strengthen us and provide comfort.

We find happiness that makes us forget that the night will come again.

Even the comforts within our hearts will fade away.

There will come a time when we rely on the fire to allow our eyes to see.

Then, we won't sleep freely, fearing the threat of wild animals.

I searched for you with great difficulty, and finally, I found you. I couldn't measure the levels of joy when you received my letter.

Tears forced their way out, opening the gates in my eyes. I tried to restrain them, but I couldn't.

I wished to express how I felt in my heart, but I hesitated after reading your emotionless letter.

I missed you so much, longing to hear you say you remembered me, but you showed no emotion in talking to me after a long time since we last met.

It's been three days since I had the chance to talk to you.

Although you left without saying goodbye, my heart still refuses to believe that you don't need me in your life.

Look, I haven't seen any of your messages, and if I don't send you a first, you won't contact me for the whole month.

How can you say you love me? You claimed to have missed me a lot and wished to see me, yet you can't even talk to me on the paper.

Perhaps you don't need anything from me. If you knew you were too busy, it would have been better not to talk about slaves at all.

You've brought back memories of the past when we were together, and then you left me to continue suffering alone.

LETTERS AIN'T WRITTEN

Was this your intention?

To seek revenge for all the times I neglected your feelings?
It's okay; I'm ready for anything.

I'd accept to be punished in any way you wish.

There are times when you wish to receive as much as you give, but it's difficult or even impossible.

This is because when you value your love for someone, they may care truly little or not at all.

When you need something from them that brings you closer, that's when they may need extraordinarily little from you or have no needs at a

LETTERS AIN'T WRITTEN

It's not because I lack piece paper or an ink,

It's not because I don't have time to write you a letter, Nor is it because I lack something to write with,

I really wish to write you a message every day, But before I start writing, my soul reproaches me,

Why do I write a message every day to someone who cannot write back, claiming they need me and love me so much?

I cannot speak for your heart if I don't utterly understand it deeply. It might be true that you love me,

but there's someone you love more,

and not a day goes by without writing or talking to them.

It could be due to the distance that caused our love to die, or because I couldn't make you see how much I love you.

That's what you should care about from now on; If you love someone and they love you back,

make sure to nurture and protect that love so that one day nothing like what happened in our love planet occurs.

The beautiful flowers we planted when we were together, flourishing and making others admire them, have withered, leaving no trace behind.

I wish to write more, but I can't.

My emotions make my eyes unable to hold back tears, and I fear I might stain my weak paper and be unable to write more.

148

I can't express how much I love you because I know you are aware of it.

It's enough now for the time when you were close to me. Let me go away from you starting now to save my heart.

can't bear this pain, and I know how hard it is to heal wounds that afflict my heart if I keep looking at the one who hurt it.

Thank you for everything you did in my life. Best wishes in your new life.

About the Author

ams Alriano Rabbit, an exciting Young Tanzanian poet, shares his life experiences about personal intelligence, purpose and relationship matters calling himself "Wordsmith Slave." Though He faced challenges in love, family, and friendships, which motivated him to tell his writing story.

He went to school in Mwanza for primary and secondary education, but his official writing journey began at the University of Dodoma (UDOM). There, he started creating art with words, expressing emotions through letters. His story comes from a heart that experienced both love and fear, touching the emotions of readers and showing a picture of his unique journey.

About the Publisher

Bongo Times Now is a Media company and publisher from Tanzania founded in 2019

9 798224 161317